Archaeology and the Ancient Past

Reyna Eisenstark

PICTURE CREDITS
Cover, page 32 © Roger Wood/Corbis; cover (inset), pages 5 (right), 12 (top), 21(top), 25 (top right), 25 (bottom left), 31 (center left), 31(bottom left), 35-c © Scala/Art Resource, NY; title page, 10 (top), 23, 35-e © Sandro Vannini/Corbis; pages 2-3, 26 (bottom) © Hulton-Deutsch Collection/Corbis; pages 5 (top), 30 (bottom left) © Michael Holford; page 5 (center left) © British Museum, London/Bridgeman Art Library; pages 5 (bottom), 9 (top), 12 (bottom), 34-c © Erich Lessing/Art Resource, NY; pages 6-7, 21 (center), 30 (top right), 35-a © Bridgeman Art Library; page 7 (camel) © Paul Hardy/Corbis; pages 7 (inset map), 18 (bottom right), 18-19 (map) Illustrations by Paul Mirocha; pages 8, 14, 16-17, 27 (top & bottom), 30 (top left), 34-b, 34-e © Kenneth Garrett/National Geographic Image Collection; page 9 (bottom) © Louvre, Paris, France/Bridgeman Art Library; pages 10 (bottom), 16 (inset), 28 (top), 29, 34-a, 35-b © Corbis; pages 11, 31 (center right), 31 (bottom right) © Archivo Iconografico, S.A./Corbis; pages 13, 35-d *Egypt of the Pharaohs* by Brian Fagan, © 2001 National Geographic Society, © photos by Kenneth Garrett; pages 15, 25 (bottom right), 34-f © Neil Beer/Corbis; page 18 (left) © Ron Watts/Corbis; pages 19, 34-d © Roger-Viollet, Paris/Bridgeman Art Library; page 20 © The Granger Collection, New York; pages 21 (bottom), 22 © Egyptian National Museum, Cairo, Egypt/Giraudon/Bridgeman Art Library; pages 22-23, 25 (top left) © The Griffith Institute, University of Oxford; 26 (top) The Metropolitan Museum of Art, Gift of Theodore M. Davis, 1909. (09.184.07) Photograph © 1978 The Metropolitan Museum of Art; page 28 (bottom & inset) © Dennis Cox/China Stock; page 30 (bottom right) © Picture Quest; page 31 (top left) © Hugh Sitton/Getty Images; 31 (top right) © Wolfgang Kaehler/Corbis; page 33 (left) *Mexico* by Kevin Supples, © 2002 National Geographic Society, photo © Kenneth Garrett; page 33 (center) *China* by Kevin Supples, © 2002 National Geographic Society, photo © Keren Su/Stone/Getty Images; page 33 (right) *Egypt* by Kevin Supples, © 2002 The National Geographic Society, photo © John Lawrence/Stone/Getty Images; page 36 © Gianni Dagli Orti/Corbis.

Produced through the worldwide resources of the National Geographic Society, John M. Fahey, Jr., President and Chief Executive Officer; Gilbert M. Grosvenor, Chairman of the Board; Nina D. Hoffman, Executive Vice President and President, Books and Education Publishing Group.

PREPARED BY NATIONAL GEOGRAPHIC SCHOOL PUBLISHING
Ericka Markman, Senior Vice President and President, Children's Books and Education Publishing Group; Steve Mico, Senior Vice President, Editorial Director, Publisher; Francis Downey, Executive Editor; Richard Easby, Editorial Manager; Anne Stone, Lori Dibble Collins, Editors; Bea Jackson, Director of Layout and Design; Jim Hiscott, Design Manager; Cynthia Olson, Art Director; Margaret Sidlosky, Illustrations Director; Matt Wascavage, Manager of Publishing Services; Sean Philpotts, Jane Ponton, Production Managers; Ted Tucker, Production Specialist.

MANUFACTURING AND QUALITY CONTROL
Christopher A. Liedel, Chief Financial Officer; Phillip L. Schlosser, Director; Clifton M. Brown III, Manager

CONSULTANT AND REVIEWER
Sam Goldberger, emeritus professor, Capital Community College, Hartford, Connecticut

◀ Howard Carter looks inside the tomb of King Tut.

Contents

BOOK DESIGN/PHOTO RESEARCH
Steve Curtis Design, Inc.

Published by the National Geographic Society
1145 17th Street N.W.
Washington, D.C. 20036-4688

ISBN 13: 978-0-7922-5462-1
ISBN 10: 0-7922-5462-7

Printed in the United States of America
03 04 05 06 07 22 21 20 19 18

Build
Background

Clues to the Past

Look at the pictures on this page. Thousands of years ago, people in Egypt played with games and toys like these. How are they like your toys and games? How are they different?

Objects like these give us clues about life in the past. What do the toys and games tell us? People long ago sometimes liked to have fun. How else can we learn about life in the past? Find out as you read this book.

object – an item that can be seen or felt

▲ A wooden toy horse

▲ A game board from ancient Egypt

▲ A doll from ancient Egypt

◀ An ancient game board shaped like a frog

1 Understand the Big Idea

Big Idea

People learn about the past in different ways.

Set Purpose

Find out three ways people learn about life in the past.

Discovering the Past in ANCIENT

Ancient Egypt was home to a great **civilization.** The people who lived there left clues about how they lived. One clue is the pyramids. These buildings have stood in the desert for thousands of years.

Who built the pyramids? Why did they build them? What is inside? Scientists and others who want to know about history ask these questions. Then they try to find the answers.

ancient — very old or from very long ago

civilization — a highly developed culture

Questions You Will Explore

What are archaeologists?

Why do they want to learn about the past?

EGYPT

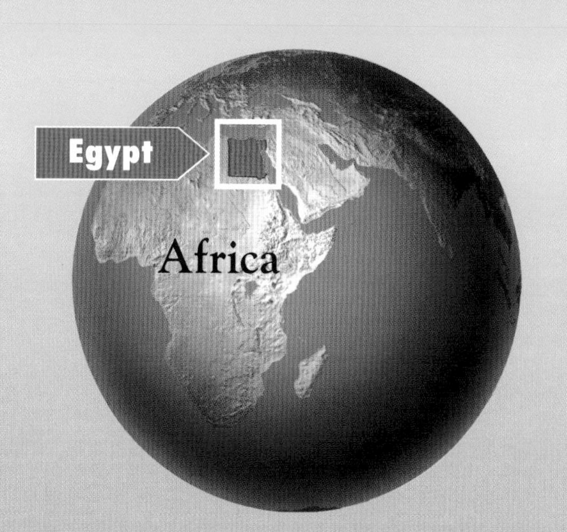

▲ These pyramids are in Giza, Egypt.

▲ This ancient Egyptian carving is being cleaned of dirt.

Digging Up the Past

Scientists who study objects from the past have a special name. They are called **archaeologists.** Archaeologists look for things that people from the past have left behind.

Archaeologists gather clues in many places. They look in old buildings. They also look for objects buried under the ground. Archaeologists often have to dig to find what they are looking for.

archaeologist — a scientist who studies what people from the past have left behind

▲ **This hippo is an artifact from ancient Egypt.**

Objects From Long Ago

The objects that archaeologists study are called **artifacts.** Artifacts are objects made by people long ago. Artifacts tell about life in ancient times.

Artifacts can take many shapes. Old toys and games are artifacts. Art, bowls, and **mummies** are also artifacts. Sometimes artifacts are broken. Archaeologists try to put the pieces back together.

artifact — an object made by people long ago

mummy — a dead body that is treated and wrapped in cloth to make it last a long time

▲ **The Egyptians made this mummy of a cat long ago.**

▲ **Pyramids are tombs built with heavy stones.**

Buildings Are Artifacts

Many artifacts are small. But ancient buildings are artifacts, too. For example, the pyramids of ancient Egypt are artifacts. Archaeologists have studied the pyramids. This is what they have learned.

- Most of the pyramids were **tombs.**
- Kings were buried inside pyramids with things they might need.
- Ancient Egyptians believed in life after death.

tomb — a place built for the dead

▼ **A king was buried in this casket.**

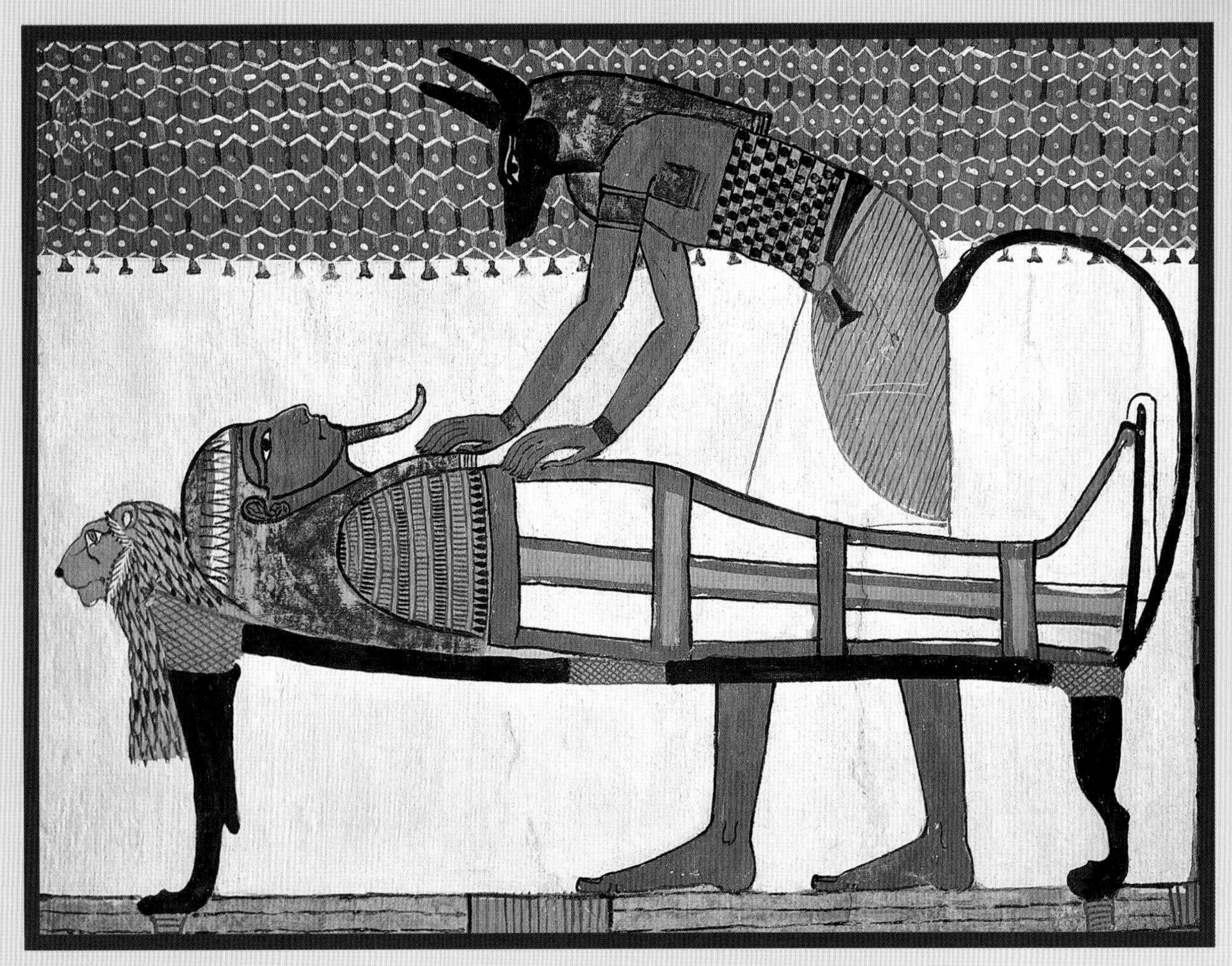

▲ **Pictures inside the pyramids tell about life in ancient Egypt.**

Ancient Art and Artifacts

Archaeologists also study art. Art tells about the past. Many Egyptian pyramids have beautiful paintings inside. These paintings are artifacts. They show what life was like long ago.

Artifacts are easier to study if they are in good condition. That is why archaeologists have learned so much from the pyramids. The rooms inside are safe from sun and rain. Pyramids have protected artifacts for many years.

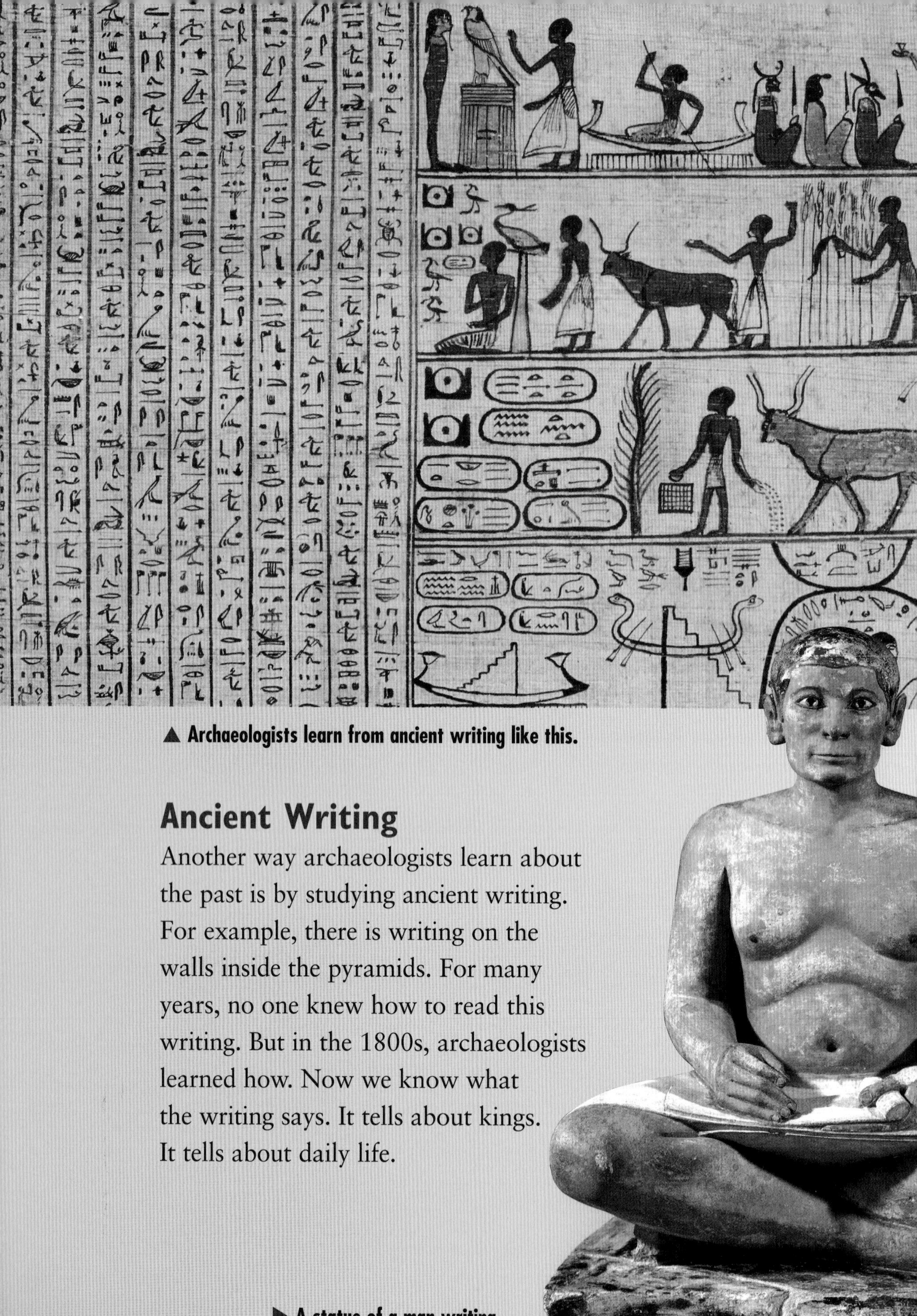

▲ Archaeologists learn from ancient writing like this.

Ancient Writing

Another way archaeologists learn about the past is by studying ancient writing. For example, there is writing on the walls inside the pyramids. For many years, no one knew how to read this writing. But in the 1800s, archaeologists learned how. Now we know what the writing says. It tells about kings. It tells about daily life.

▶ A statue of a man writing

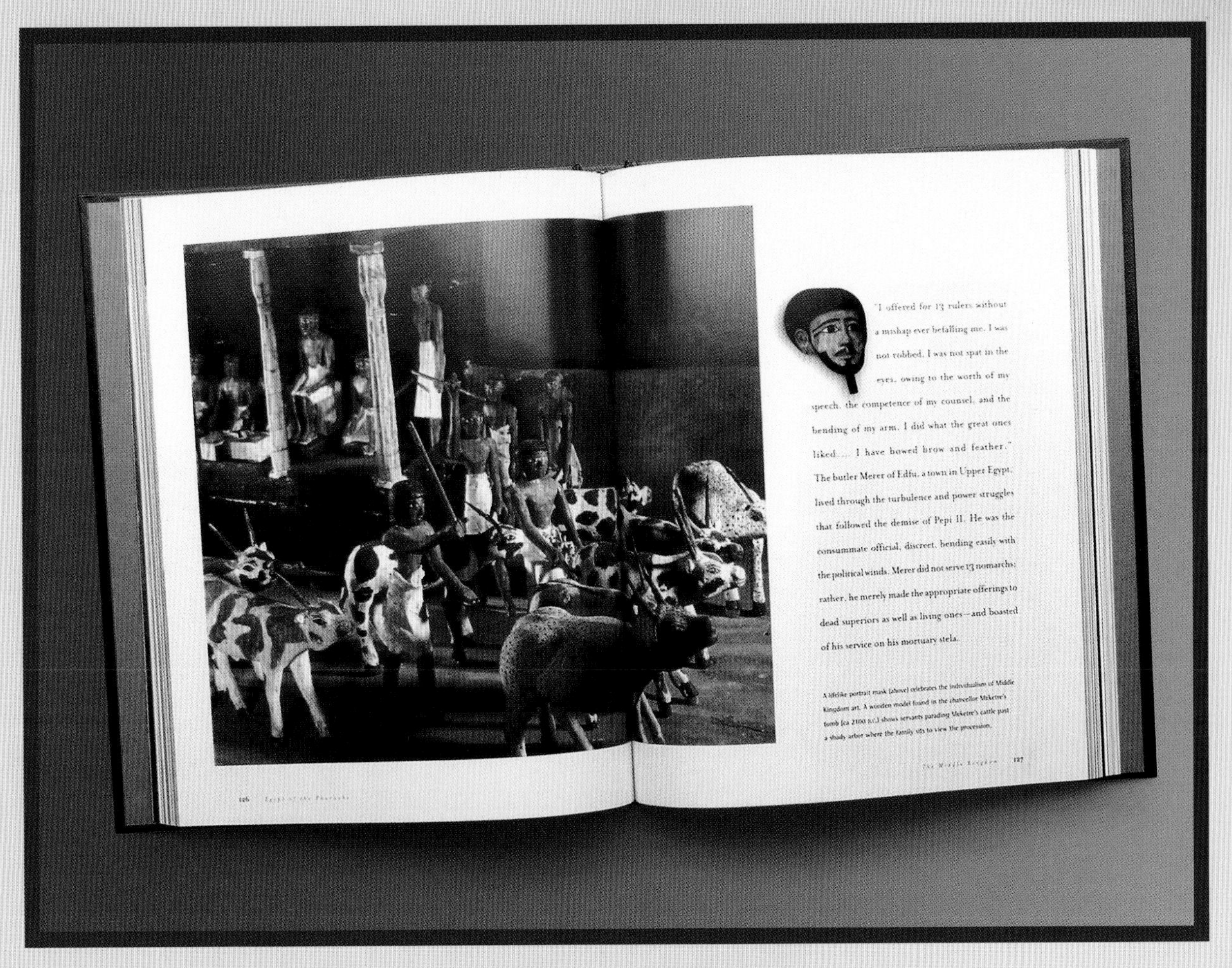

"I offered for 13 rulers without a mishap ever befalling me. I was not robbed. I was not spat in the eyes, owing to the worth of my speech, the competence of my counsel, and the bending of my arm. I did what the great ones liked.... I have bowed brow and feather." The butler Merer of Edfu, a town in Upper Egypt, lived through the turbulence and power struggles that followed the demise of Pepi II. He was the consummate official, discreet, bending easily with the political winds. Merer did not serve 13 nomarchs; rather, he merely made the appropriate offerings to dead superiors as well as living ones—and boasted of his service on his mortuary stela.

A lifelike portrait mask (above) celebrates the individualism of Middle Kingdom art. A wooden model found in the chancellor Meketre's tomb (ca 2100 B.C.) shows servants parading Meketre's cattle past a shady arbor where the family sits to view the procession.

127

▲ **Archaeologists learn about the past by reading books.**

Written Sources

Sometimes archaeologists read **primary sources.** These are written by someone who saw an event or who lived at the time. Other writings are called **secondary sources.** A secondary source is written by someone who was not there at the time. Both kinds of sources help archaeologists learn about the past.

primary source — a record of an event written by someone who was actually there

secondary source — a record of an event written long after or by someone who was not there

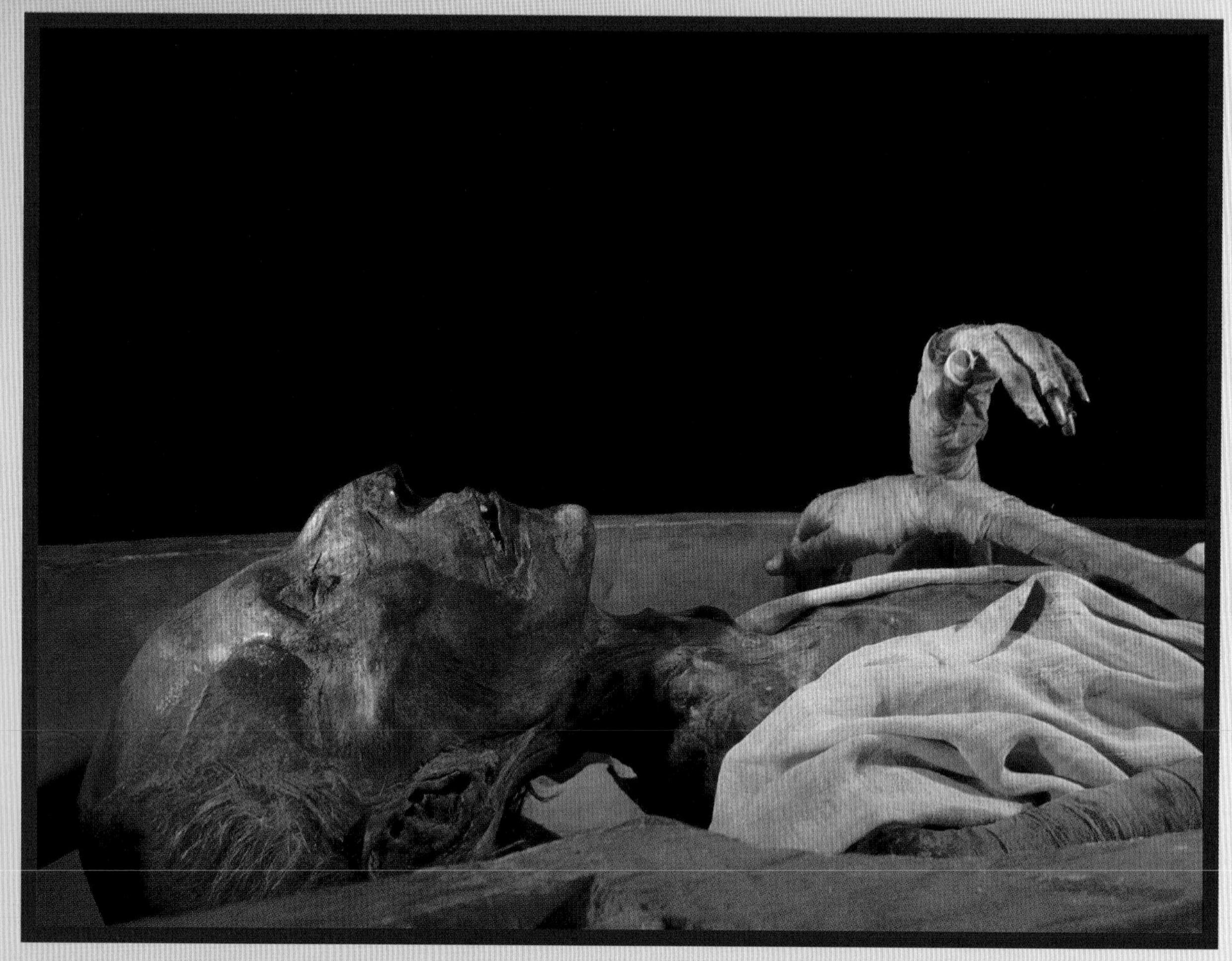

▲ **Museums preserve mummies like this one in special cases.**

Protecting Artifacts

Archaeologists often look for new artifacts to study. But they can also learn from artifacts found by others. This is why we need to protect artifacts.

Museums have special rooms and equipment. These keep artifacts safe. Museums store mummies in special cases. Museums **preserve** artifacts for people in the future.

museum — a place where artifacts, art, and other objects are kept for people to see

preserve — to keep safe

▲ **People visit museums to see artifacts and learn about the past.**

Museums Tell About the Past

Museums do more than protect artifacts. They also let people look at what archaeologists have found. People visit museums to see ancient artifacts.

Some museums have libraries. People go to museums to read about life in ancient times. Museums are another way for us to learn about life in the past.

Stop and Think!

Name three ways people can learn about the past.

2 Take a Closer Look

Recap

Explain how people learn about the past.

Set Purpose

Read how one archaeologist learned about ancient Egypt.

▲ Howard Carter

Uncovering King

In 1917, Howard Carter traveled thousands of miles to Egypt. Then he traveled back thousands of years in time.

Carter was an archaeologist. He was searching for an ancient tomb. He knew that inside the tomb he would find clues about a time long ago.

Tut

Lost Treasures

Kings in ancient Egypt were buried in special tombs. Some tombs were in pyramids. Others were in a place called the Valley of the Kings. Many archaeologists wanted to find these tombs. They wanted to study the valuable artifacts inside. But often there was nothing left. People had stolen the treasures long before.

▲ **Archaeologists dig for artifacts.**

Ancien

Mediterranean Sea

Pyramids

● **Archaeological sites**

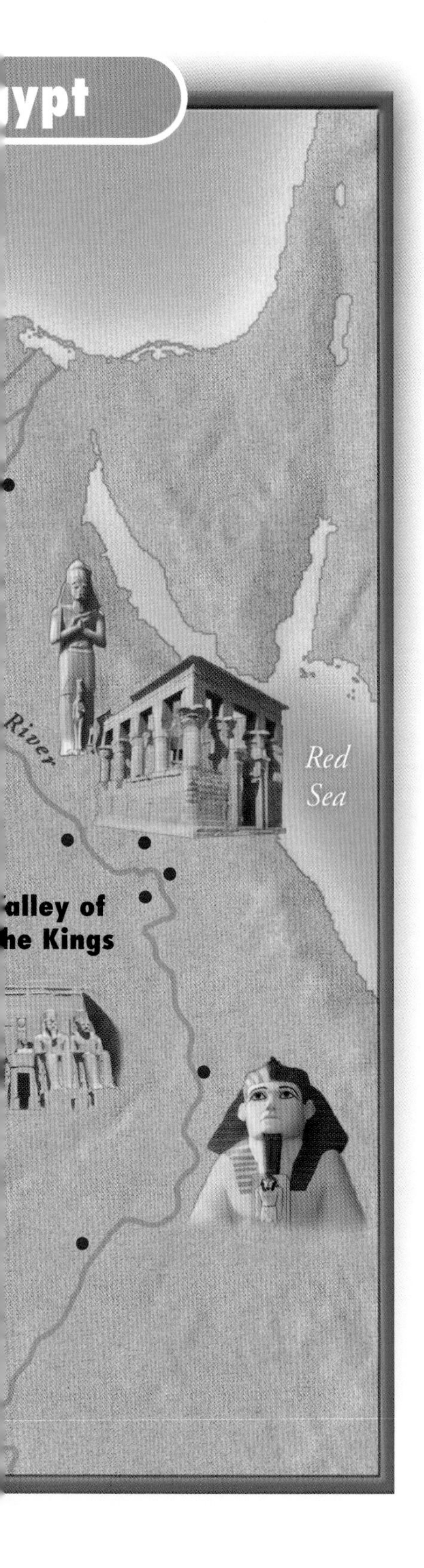

Looking for King Tut

Howard Carter had a plan. He read stories of Egypt's history. He learned about a leader named Tutankhamun, or King Tut. No one knew where King Tut was buried.

Carter wanted to look for King Tut's tomb. He decided to look in the Valley of the Kings. Carter got a map of the valley. On the map, he marked the tombs that had already been found. Carter thought King Tut's tomb might be nearby. He began to dig in 1917.

▲ **Carter and his team dig in search of King Tut.**

Stairs to a Door

Carter searched for many years. He found nothing. But he kept looking. He was determined to find King Tut's tomb. On November 4, 1922, his luck changed. Carter's team discovered a step cut into some rock.

The team kept digging. Soon they found fifteen more steps. The steps led to an ancient doorway. The door seemed to be sealed. It had the name Tutankhamun written on it.

▼ **Carter and his team entered the tomb through this door.**

The Room Beyond

The team took nearly three weeks to clear the staircase. Carter slowly made a hole in the door. He was stunned by what he found. Through the door was a series of rooms. One room held King Tut's mummy. Other rooms were filled with artifacts. These artifacts had been buried with King Tut thousands of years before.

▼ **This is a chair from King Tut's tomb.**

▲ **The Egyptians believed this statue would protect King Tut.**

▶ **A statue of young King Tut**

The Glint of Gold!

The ancient tomb held over 3,500 artifacts. It held jewels, statues, and paintings. It also held lots of gold. King Tut had a solid gold coffin. He had a gold mask and a gold throne.

Howard Carter carefully studied all these artifacts. They showed the great riches of Egyptian kings. They also told about Egyptian life. It took Carter ten years to finish work on King Tut's tomb.

▼ **A mask for King Tut's mummy**

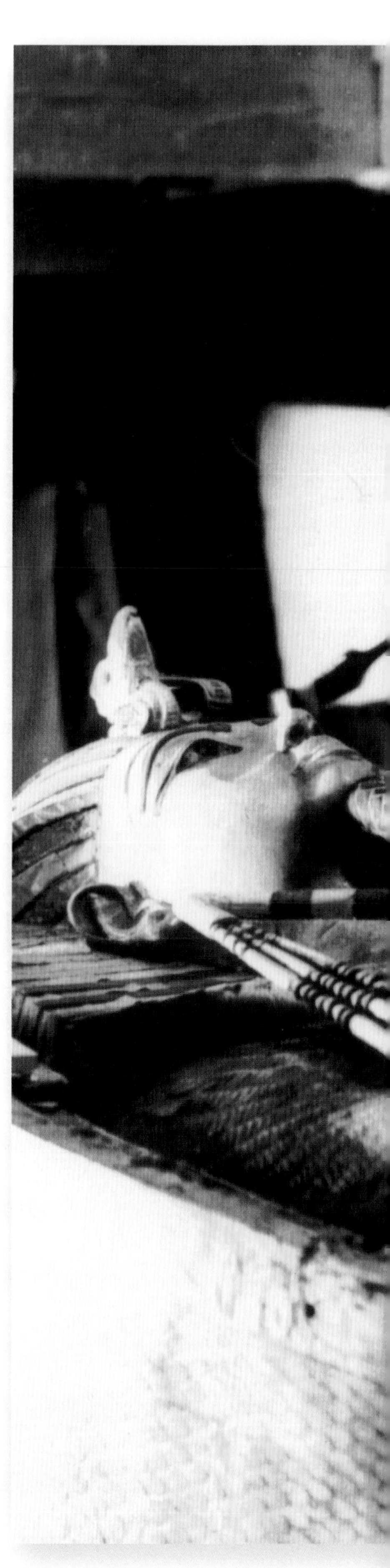

▶ **Howard Carter uses a brush to clean an artifact.**

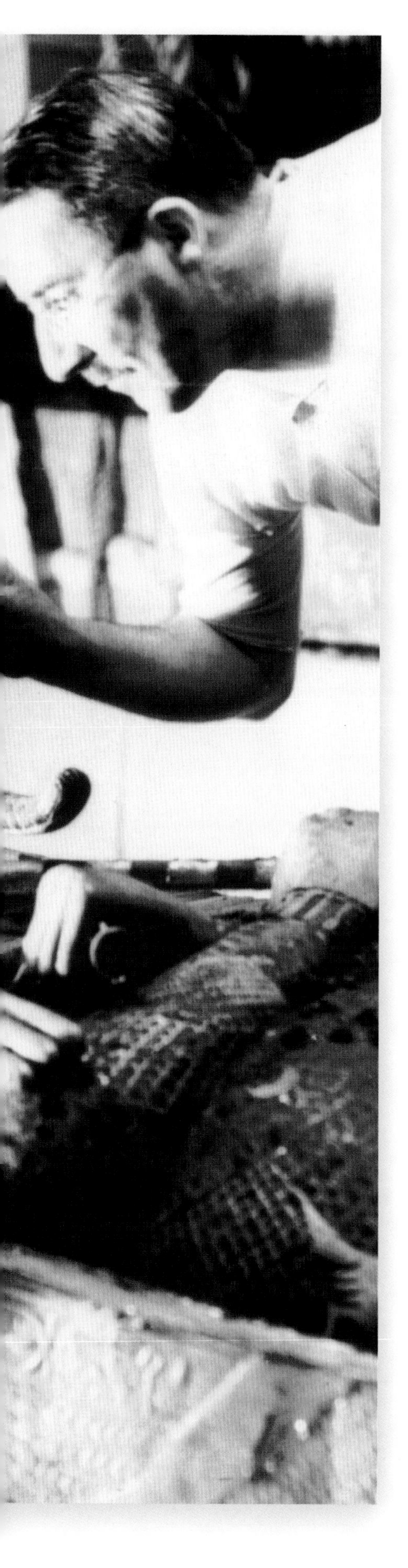

A Famous King

King Tut died more than 3,000 years ago. Yet he is well known today. Why? Howard Carter's amazing discovery made King Tut famous.

King Tut's tomb has taught us a lot about life in ancient Egypt. The tomb shows that people believed in life after death. It also shows that people honored their king. And it shows the great riches of the ancient Egyptian civilization.

King Tut's golden throne

Stop and Think!

How did Howard Carter learn about Egypt?

3 Make **Connections**

Recap

Describe how Howard Carter uncovered Egypt's past.

Set Purpose

Read more about archaeology and ancient Egypt.

CONNECT WHAT YOU HAVE LEARNED

Archaeology and the Ancient Past

People lived long ago in ancient Egypt. They left clues about how they lived. These clues help archaeologists find out what life was like in ancient times.

Here are some ideas that you learned about archaeologists.

- Archaeologists study things that people from the past have left behind.
- Archaeologists look for artifacts.
- Archaeologists read books and ancient writings.
- Museums help archaeologists and others learn about the ancient past.

Check What You Have Learned

HOW do people learn about life in the ancient past?

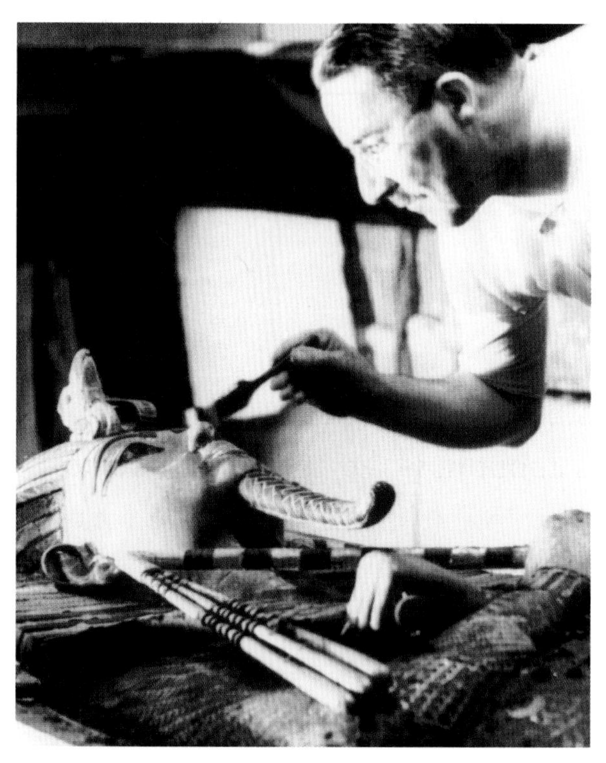

▲ Howard Carter studied artifacts that he found in King Tut's tomb.

▲ Artifacts come in many shapes and sizes.

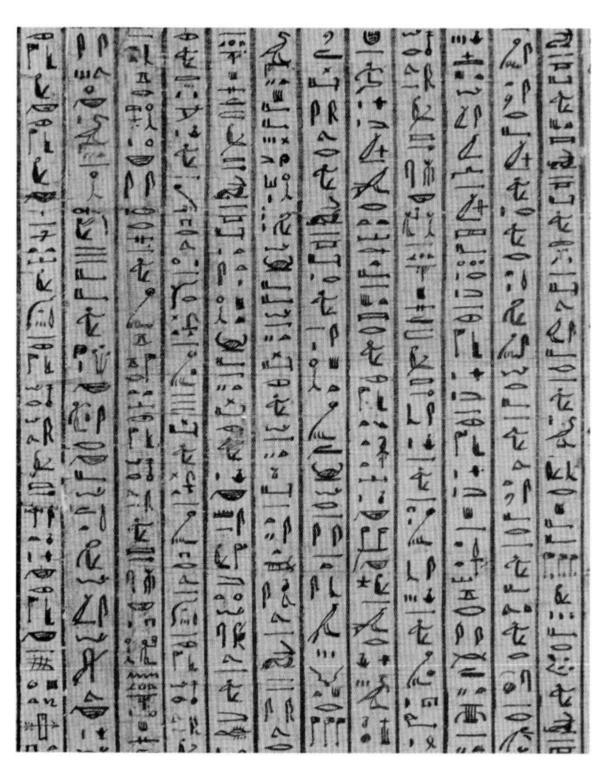

▲ The ancient Egyptians wrote about their kings and daily life.

▲ People visit museums to see mummies and other artifacts from long ago.

Finding the Tomb

How did Howard Carter know where to find King Tut's tomb? He could have spent years looking for it in the wrong place. Instead, he studied other artifacts.

An American named Theodore Davis had found some ancient Egyptian jars. The jars had the name Tutankhamun on them. Davis found them in the Valley of the Kings. That is how Carter knew that King Tut was buried nearby.

▶ A jar like this helped Howard Carter find King Tut's tomb.

◀ Workers carry artifacts from King Tut's tomb.

Dr. Zahi Hawass and his team study an ancient tomb.

Dr. Zahi Hawass

Dr. Zahi Hawass

Dr. Zahi Hawass is a famous archaeologist. Some people call him "Mr. Pyramid." Hawass has found many ancient tombs in Egypt. He has learned that people from all over Egypt helped to build the pyramids. Some people hauled the heavy stones into place. Others sent food for the workers. It took many people to build the pyramids!

Pyramids Tell a Story

Egypt was not the only ancient kingdom to build pyramids. The Maya built pyramids, too. The Maya lived in what is now Mexico. Both the Maya and the Egyptians buried their rulers in pyramids. The Maya built rooms at the top of many pyramids. People can still climb the steep stairs to reach these rooms.

▲ **A pyramid built by the ancient Maya**

▲ **Clay soldiers from the tomb of Qin Shi Huang Di in China**

▼ A Maya temple in Mexico

CONNECT TO ANCIENT CHINA

An Army in the Tomb

Qin Shi Huang Di was China's first king. He wanted an army to protect him after he died. So he made an army out of clay. The army had thousands of soldiers and horses. They were all made out of clay. When the king died, the army of clay was buried with him. People soon forgot about the clay army. But in 1974 some farmers found the king's tomb. Now people visit his clay soldiers in museums.

Zoom in on Words

Many kinds of words are used in this book. Here you will learn about words that are opposites. You will also learn about words that describe a person, place, or thing.

Antonyms

An antonym is a word that means the opposite of another word. Look at the pairs of words below. What other antonyms do you know?

Artifacts can be **small** objects like bowls or beads.

Artifacts can also be **large** buildings like the pyramids.

Long ago, Egyptians played with **ancient** games and toys.

Some **modern** games and toys look like ones from ancient Egypt.

Adjectives

An adjective is a word that describes a person, place, or thing. An adjective often goes before the word it describes. Find the adjectives below and use them in sentences of your own.

People look for artifacts in **old** buildings such as the pyramids.

Archaeologists put **broken** artifacts back together.

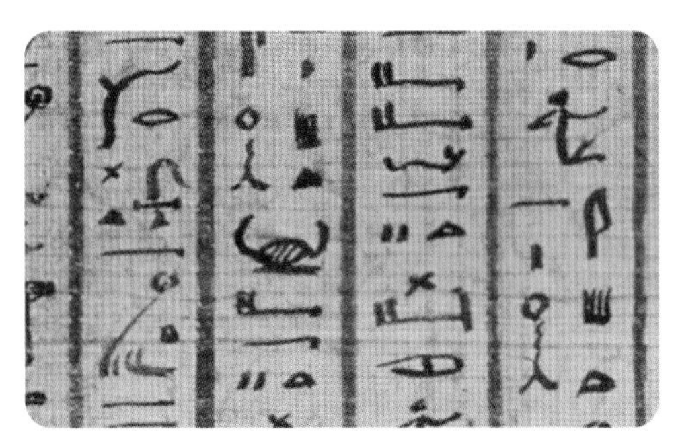

Archaeologists study **ancient** writing.

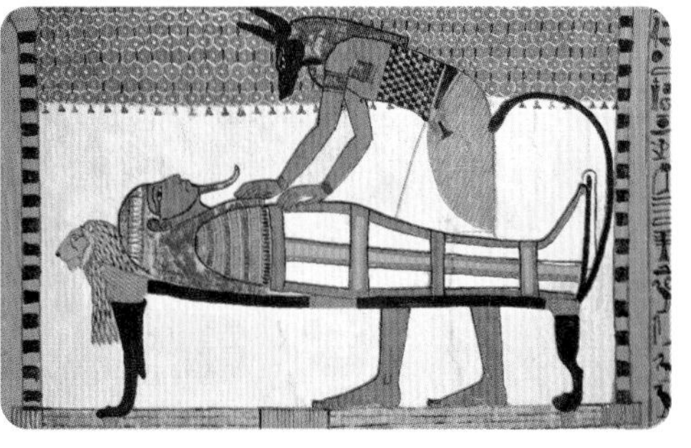

Many Egyptian pyramids have **beautiful** paintings inside them.

The kings were buried with gold, jewels, and other **valuable** things.

King Tut had a **gold** mask and throne.

Research and Write

Write About Ancient Egypt

Learn more about the treasures of King Tut. What else did Howard Carter find in the tomb? What do these artifacts tell you about life in ancient Egypt?

Research

Collect books and reference materials, or go online.

Read and Take Notes

As you read, take notes and draw pictures.

Write

Pretend you work in a museum. Artifacts from King Tut's tomb will be on display in your museum. Write a brochure telling people about the treasures they will see.

Read and Compare

Read More About the Ancient Past

Find and read other books about people in the ancient past. As you read, think about these questions.

- What is special about this ancient culture?
- How was life in ancient times like life today?
- How was it different?

Books to Read

▲ **Find out more about the people of Egypt, past and present.**

▲ **Learn about the Maya and ancient times in Mexico.**

▲ **Discover the roots of Chinese culture long ago.**

Glossary

ancient (page 6)
Very old or from very long ago
Egypt has many ancient buildings.

KEY CONCEPT

archaeologist (page 8)
A scientist who studies what people from the past have left behind
Archaeologists look for clues about life in the past.

KEY CONCEPT

artifact (page 9)
An object made by people long ago
Artifacts can tell us about life in ancient times.

civilization (page 6)
A highly developed culture
Many archaeologists study the civilization of ancient Egypt.

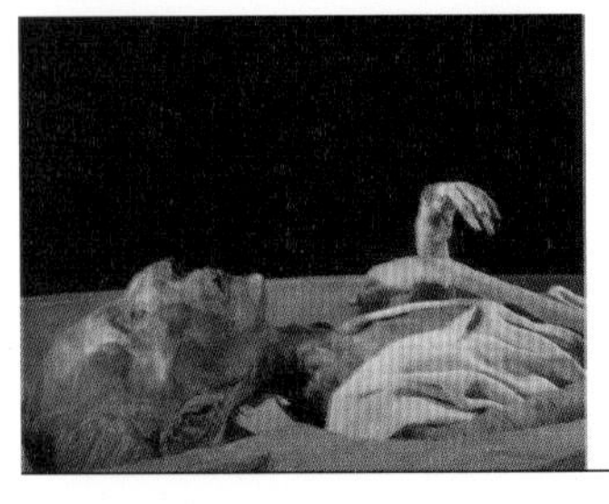

mummy (page 9)
A dead body that is treated and wrapped in cloth to make it last a long time
A mummy is an artifact from ancient Egypt.

KEY CONCEPT

museum (page 14)
A place where artifacts, art, and other objects are kept for people to see
A museum helps people learn about ancient ways of life.

object (page 4)
An item that can be seen or felt
Archaeologists learn by studying objects that people leave behind.

preserve (page 14)
To keep safe
Museums help preserve objects from the past.

primary source (page 13)
A record of an event written by someone who was actually there
Primary sources sometimes tell about daily life.

secondary source (page 13)
A record of an event written long after or by someone who was not there
Secondary sources are one way to learn about the past.

tomb (page 10)
A place built for the dead
Egyptian kings were buried in tombs made of heavy stone.

Index